Cover painting *A Cottage Garden* A. Wilkinson
Facing page *A Cheshire Cottage* A.C. Strachan

Illustrations Fine Art Photographic, London

Design Alison Jewell

Picture Research Fleur Robertson

Production Ruth Arthur
            Sally Connolly
            Neil Randles
            Jonathan Tickner

Director of Production Gerald Hughes

Published in 1994 by CLB Publishing
for Selecta Book Ltd, Devizes
CLB 4238
© 1994 CLB Publishing Ltd, Godalming, Surrey
All rights reserved
Printed and bound in Spain by Gráficas Estella, S.A. Navarra.
ISBN 1 85833 179 X

THE
COTTAGE HOMES
BIRTHDAY BOOK

SELECT
EDITIONS

January

Punting on the River (detail) A.C. Strachan

JANUARY

1

2

3

4

5

6

7

8

9

10

A Cottage Garden with Hollyhocks J. Fisher

JANUARY

11

12

13

14

15

16

17

18

19

20

Punting on the River A.C. Strachan

JANUARY

21

22

23

24

25

26

27

28

29

30/31

Cernaes Bay, North Wales T.N. Smith

February

By *the Cottage Door* (detail) A.C. Strachan

February

1

2

3

4

5

6

7

8

9

10

FEBRUARY

11

12

13

14

15

16

17

18

19

20

FEBRUARY

21

22

23

24

25

26

27

28

29

By the Cottage Door A.C. Strachan

March

Crossing the Ford (detail) A.C. Strachan

MARCH

1

2

3

4

5

6

7

8

9

10

The Butterfly H. Allingham

MARCH

11

12

13

14

15

16

17

18

19

20

Cottage at Clifton D. Woodlock

MARCH

21

22

23

24

25

26

27

28

29

30/31

Crossing the Ford A.C. Strachan

April

A *Stream by a Cottage Door* (detail) A.C. Strachan

APRIL

1

2

3

4

5

6

7

8

9

10

APRIL

11

12

13

14

15

16

17

18

19

20

APRIL

21

22

23

24

25

26

27

28

29

30

A Stream by a Cottage Door, Ockley, Surrey A.C. Strachan

May

Peeling Potatoes (detail) E. Walbourn

MAY

1

2

3

4

5

6

7

8

9

10

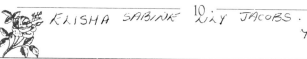
ELISHA SABINE   LILY JACOBS. 10/5/97
                 4 NB. H.25.

Spring Blossom H. Allingham

MAY

11

12

13

14

15

16

17

18

19

20

Peeling Potatoes (detail) E. Walbourn

MAY

21

22

23

24

25

26

27

28

29

30/31

Cernaes Bay, North Wales (detail) A.E. Brockbank

June

A Cottage Garden, Dorset (detail) T.N. Smith

JUNE

1

2

3

4

5

6

7

8

9

10

JANRT & BRUCE CORES WEDDING ANN.
RUBY - 1994.

JUNE

11

12

13

14

15

16

17

18

19

20

JUNE

—————————————— 21 ——————————————

—————————————— 22 ——————————————

—————————————— 23 ——————————————

—————————————— 24 ——————————————

—————————————— 25 ——————————————

—————————————— 26 ——————————————

—————————————— 27 ——————————————

—————————————— 28 ——————————————

—————————————— 29 ——————————————

—————————————— 30 ——————————————

A Cottage Garden, Dorset T.N. Smith

July

At Madehurst, Sussex (detail) J. Matthews

JULY

1

2

3

4

5

6

7

8

9

10

In the Cottage Garden, Alveston A.C. Strachan

JULY

11

12

13

NRU & DAWN'S
WEDDING ANNIVERSARY

14

15

16

17

18

19

20

At Madehurst, Sussex J. Matthews

JULY

21

22

Joya + George - Golden
Wedding Anniversary - 2009

23

24

25

FREYA AMBER
ELIZABETH JACOBS

26

27

28

29

30/31

Daisies by the Cottage Door T. MacKay

August

The Cottage Guard (detail) A.C. Strachan

AUGUST

1

2

3

4

5

6

7

8

9

10

The Cottage Guard A.C. Strachan

AUGUST

11

12

13

14

15

16

17

18

19

20

The Runaway H. Allingham

AUGUST

21

22

23

24

25

26

27

28

29

30/31

Cottages on the River A.C. Strachan

September

On the Cottage Steps (detail) A.C. Strachan

SEPTEMBER

1

2

3

4

5

6

7

8

9

10

SEPTEMBER

11

12

13

14

15

16

17

18

19

20

SEPTEMBER

21

22

23

24

25

26

27

28

29

30

On the Cottage Steps A.C. Strachan

October

Outside a Country Cottage (detail) T.N. Smith

OCTOBER

1

2

3

4

5

6

7

8

9

10

East End Farm, Moss Lane, Pinner H. Allingham

OCTOBER

11

12

13

14

15

16

17

18

19

20

Outside a Country Cottage T.N. Smith

OCTOBER

21

22

23

24

25

26

27

28

29

30/31

Haven on the Hill A.C. Strachan

November

At the Cottage Gate (detail) H. Allingham

NOVEMBER

1

2

3

4

5

6

7

8

9

10

November

11

12

13

14

15
EDWIN FRANCIS JACOBS -
1996

16

17

18

19

20

NOVEMBER

21

22

23

24

25

26

27

28

29

30

At the Cottage Gate H. Allingham

December

A Picturesque Cottage Garden (detail) A.C. Strachan

December

1

2

3

4

5

6

7

8

9

10

A Sunny Cottage J. Kirkpatrick

DECEMBER

11

12

13

14

15

16

17

18

19

20

A Picturesque Cottage Garden A.C. Strachan

December

JOYCE & PHIN —
GOLDEN WEDDING 1996

21

22

23

24

25

26

27

28

29

30/31

A Cottage Garden A. Wilkinson

NOTES

NOTES